Blanche Rose

Little Rose Girl

By

Lynne Turnbow

JANAWAY PUBLISHING, INC.
Santa Maria, California
2011

Published by:

Janaway Publishing, Inc.
732 Kelsey Ct.
Santa Maria, California 93454
(805) 925-1038
www.janawaygenealogy.com

2011

ISBN: 978-1-59641-250-7

This Book is Dedicated to my Beloved Aunt
Violet, who shows me everyday
what it means to live with Courage

CONTENTS

PREFACE

For as long as I can remember, I have always felt that my mother's story should be told. The events of her life were deeply entwined with the significant period of history during which she lived. This is the story of a little girl who grew up during the Great Depression, experienced the heart-rending events of World War II, and lived to see the United States send rockets into outer space. But more importantly, this is the story of a woman with great courage, love and fortitude, who took the challenges that life handed to her and found a way to become strengthened through adversity, and still believe that love and joy were possible.

Most of us live our lives without fully realizing the far reaching effect our influence may have on others. I am sure during her life she would never have imagined that one day her daughter would write a book about the sometimes ordinary, and sometimes extraordinary, events of her journey. It is my honor to share her story with you, in the hopes that it will enrich your life as it has mine.

Lynne Turnbow
San Luis Obispo, California
November 1, 2011

CHAPTER ONE: MIRACLE BABY

A cold, blustery wind blew through the mountains. A young girl sat on the porch, with the dark night sky stretching out as far as she could see. The stars that illuminated the sky by the millions did little to calm her fears and anguish, as she heard her mother scream out in pain. Over and over she listened, as fear and helplessness crowded in around her. Her brother, James Truman, sat quietly nearby. They waited together, as they often did. They understood that their world, as they knew it, hung suspended, between what they had known, and this horrible night that wasn't supposed to happen. Yet, life had brought this unexpected, premature labor to their mother, and, as she labored, they waited, cried, and they knew fear.

It was 1933, the height of the Great Depression. Twelve-year-old Blanche and her older brother tried to understand what was happening in their mother's bedroom, as she labored two months prematurely, with a small-town doctor attending the birth, their Aunt Liddy and older sister, sixteen-year-old Violet, at her bedside. How long it went on seemed to become like a void in the night expanse of darkness and space, and then, suddenly, it grew quiet. Too quiet. Their mother's voice grew silent, and there was a heaviness that seemed to descend and surround them. In the room, they could hear people shuffling about, and something that sounded like a young kitten softly making noise.   They huddled closer to one another on the wood steps of the porch, and confusion lingered, as they tried to make sense out of what might be happening inside the house.

Finally, they heard footsteps approaching as the screen door squeaked, and their Father, Dana Rose, walked closer to them. His face was twisted in pain, as he tried to make the words come out of his mouth. It seemed as if days passed before he finally spoke. "Your mother has died," he said with a broken voice. James and Blanche looked at each other in disbelief. There had to be a mistake. Mama had always been there for them. Though they were poor and struggling, as were most of the farmers and ranch families in the valley, they always had mother's smile, love and reassurance at the end of the day, to make them believe things really were not so bad. Mama made everything alright. It was impossible that she could have died.

They ran to their father, and he embraced them, and then began to speak in a voice that made them know that nothing would ever be the same again. "The baby is still alive," he said in a raspy voice, "but just barely. The doctor says there is no hope for a child born this young. Aunt Liddy is with the baby now." Blanche's mind was a tumble of fragmented thoughts, emotion, confusion, disbelief and grief. After a few silent minutes, Father turned and went back inside the house. They could hear him wake their younger sister June, who was asleep on the hard couch, and her stifled cry, as he told her that she no longer had a mother. They went inside to sit near her, and try to find some balance in a world that had just spiraled out of control.

A deafening silence filled their world as they waited. Finally, they heard the sound of the bedroom door open, and Aunt Liddy emerged holding something so tiny in her arms, they couldn't conceive what it could be. "This is your sister," she said softly to them. "Her name is Melba, and her middle name will be Maude, after your mother, and," she continued, "she will live." That being said, she walked into the kitchen towards the wood-burning stove, the only source of heat in the house. "Come closer, children," she gently called out to them. "Your sister has been born very early," she said, "and she isn't going to look like most of the babies that you have seen when you look at her. But this baby is your blood and my sister's child, and come Heaven or Earth, she is going to live!"

Blanche felt as if she existed in a haze, as days and weeks slipped by. Time had no continuity, as she learned to live without her mother's affection and assurance. Aunt Liddy was a constant in their lives now, as she sat by the warm stove for hours, rocking and cooing to her tiniest niece and feeding her from an eyedropper. Baby Melba had no eyebrows or eyelashes due to her prematurity, and they made a tiny bed for her in a shoebox. Aunt Liddy said she needed to feel enclosed in a tiny space, to take the place of her mother's womb. Blanche, Violet, James and June adored their new sister, but fear was a constant guest, as they thought of how easily she could die, just as their mother had. Neighbors throughout the small farming community stopped by the farmhouse often to bring food to the desolated family, and to help in any way that they could. Violet and Blanche not only lost their mother that day, they lost what was left of their childhood. On that day, they both became not only older sisters, they became mothers to their tiny sibling.

Violet and Blanche took turns holding the baby for hours, rocking and singing, willing this infant to fight for life, and slowly tiny Melba Maude began to gain weight. Never could there have been a baby more loved. Despite all logical medical predictions, a beautiful baby girl began to grow and thrive.

Blanche hurried home from the one-room schoolhouse that she attended during the day with the other children from the valley. She was working on a beautiful dress for baby Melba, and wanted to spend some time working on the tiny hand stitches she laboriously poured into the garment before the last hours of daylight disappeared, and it would be so much harder to see by the oil lamp. When she entered the house, Violet was in the kitchen cooking dinner, and Aunt Liddy was rocking the baby. She walked over and put her little finger near Melba, who joyfully grabbed it and squealed with delight from the attention of her older sister. Blanche and Violet smiled and, as time passed, some degree of perspective began to slowly settle over the family, as they learned to live with their loss and to find purpose in living, not only for themselves, but to raise this blessed child that their mother had died giving birth to.

As months turned into years, baby Melba learned to walk and talk, and was the light which illuminated the Rose family. Blanche often anguished as she looked at Melba and wondered about her own future. The small one-room schoolhouse in the valley only provided education through the eighth grade. To finish High School, she would have to move to Provo and live with her Grandma Maxwell, her Father's mother. A fiery little lady of Irish descent, her Grandmother had been Jennie O'Dell before she married. Provo was more than two hours away from the quiet farming community where she had grown up, and if she moved, she would no longer be able to see Melba everyday, and the thought of that pained her deeply.

It was Saturday afternoon, and Blanche and Violet had been cooking and cleaning, making the most of the humble home that they lived in. A car slowly pulled up in front of the house, and Dad emerged with a woman who looked somewhat familiar to them. They stepped out on the porch, and Melba tottered after them. Dad walked in front of the car, looked over at them and then spoke, "This is your new mother," was all he said. Once again, life had changed forever.

CHAPTER TWO: THE CITY

In the coming years, Blanche worked hard at completing her education in Provo, and finding a way back to the farm to see Melba as often as she could. She was very protective of her precious younger sister, and determined to survive in her life, and to find a way to be able to provide a home for Melba at some point in the future.

Provo was very different from the farm and the life she had known during the first fourteen years of her life. There was not only more education available, but there were stores, books, movies and experiences that expanded her world. After four years with Grandma Maxwell, Blanche graduated from high school, and began working at a new store in town named Woolworths.

Blanche was a beautiful young woman with dark hair and a petite figure. She had always done well in math, and her intelligence and warm personality helped her to become a valuable part of the department store work force. Her supervisor often expressed how much he appreciated her hard work, and her willingness to help customers and co-workers with whatever they needed. Blanche had grown wise beyond her years at a very young age.

As time passed, she began to notice, with a new interest, the charming and handsome young man who seemed to linger a little longer during the work day, when he came to speak to her about work-related subjects. His name was Edward, and Blanche began to feel something special when she was in his presence, and with their easy, effortless conversations. Eventually, they began to get dinner together after work, and to find much more to talk about than their shared place of employment. Like a warm whisper, Love came into her life, and for the first time in many years, she found a place of trust and comfort with Ed in her life.

The year was 1942. World War II had sent the world into a catastrophic plunge of conflict, cruelty and chaos. Hitler boldly declared that one day he would rule the world from the steps of the White House. Men, in those days, wanted to fight in the war. Many Americans had been lost at Pearl Harbor, and throughout the world, people heard of atrocities committed by the Nazi's that defied belief. Edward and Blanche married that year. While the world spun out of control, their world, as it existed when they were together, was a place of safety and security that she had never known before. Ed was an articulate, intelligent and kind man. He joined the Air Force and began his military training. He deeply loved his wife, and the days were never long enough when he was able to get leave, and spend his days of R and R with her. Their first anniversary was approaching, and the time seemed to be passing so quickly. Soon he would be finished with his training and, without doubt, would be stationed somewhere where violence and death were constant.

Blanche glanced at the clock, and her heart was light. In a few minutes, she would be leaving work and heading to the train station to meet Ed for his weekend leave. He was flying his last training mission, and then was coming home before he received his orders to ship out. After putting the last of her day's work in order, Blanche reached for her black wool coat and slipped her hands into her black leather gloves. She was strikingly beautiful, and her inner happiness shone forth from within her. She picked up her purse and started towards the door, when, suddenly, she stopped as if she had been stabbed in the stomach. The door opened, and two men in military uniforms soberly walked into her office. They were holding a yellow telegram in their hands, and they looked at her and said, "We're looking for Mrs. Edward Reynolds."

"Oh, please God no," she cried. "Anything but this. You couldn't take another person from me, who I love this much," she tried to reason with God. But there was no mistake about the truth that lay inside the envelope. Edward had crashed on his last training flight and was dead.

In the days that followed, she tried to get information about what had happened during this standard training drill. It was a freak accident. There had been trouble up ahead, a miscalculation on someone's part about the nearness of the next mountain range. Had he ejected from the plane immediately, he would have lived. But Edward knew that there were other planes behind him, and in the precious seconds that he took to radio, "Mayday, Mayday, change course, critical trouble ahead," he had lost his window of opportunity to live, and it was too late. His plane lunged into a rapid descent towards the ground, as the planes behind him immediately changed course. No one in the successive planes was injured or killed.

Blanche lived in a dark state of shock for weeks, perhaps it was even months. She had no concept of time. On a windy, gray day, she walked to her mailbox, and inside she found a military envelope. She opened it, and realized the letter had been sent from Edward's Commanding Officer. Her eyes scanned the handwritten letter, and she realized that a kind and compassionate man had taken the time to care about her deep grief. In the final paragraph, his C.O. said that it was imperative that she know that Edward had died, because he took the time to radio to the other men in his unit of the impending danger. "You must know, Mrs. Reynolds, that Edward died that others might live."

This information did not begin to fill the enormous vacancy that had been ripped into her heart, but, somehow, understanding this part of the accident gave some sort of comfort. In the coming weeks, the inscription would be written upon his tombstone, "He died that others might live."

CHAPTER THREE: WAR

The war raged on. Country after country fell under the control of the Nazi regime, and the horrific atrocities that were sometimes written about in the paper, seemed too inconceivable to believe. By this time, Blanche's brother, James Truman, or J.T., as he was so often called, was deep into the fighting in Europe. She had been receiving letters from him since his days in basic training, and she prayed mighty prayers for his safety.

There was an army recruiting office three blocks from where Blanche lived, and she often walked by it during her daily walks, when she willed herself to get outside, breathe the air, and try to remember that she was still alive, and must make decisions about her future and moving forward in her life. She began to stop for a few seconds each day and read the posters, which were boldly plastered on the office windows. She began to think about making a change in her life, a really big change. Everywhere she looked in Provo reminded her of Ed, and of the life and future that she had lost. She was blind with grief. Slowly, she began to consider leaving the whole State of Utah behind for a while. She gradually began to consider joining the army. Women in the army were called WACS in those days, short for Women's Army Corp.

By this point in time, her sister Violet had married, and a young schoolgirl, Melba, lived with her. She knew that if she were stationed in Europe, there would be a chance of her finding and seeing her brother J.T. Ultimately, her thoughts became clear, and her decision was made. She was joining the army.

CHAPTER FOUR: SHIPPING OUT

Basic training was rough and rigorous. In many ways it was a blessing, because she was so tired by the time that she hit her bunk at night, that sleep came quickly, and the exhaustion was a relief from the intense grief that had compelled her to join up. Two more weeks were left before they were issued new clothing, and assigned to the first post that would officially begin her army career.

Blanche held the envelope in her hands for several minutes, before she carefully opened it. She knew that her assignments in the army would change her life, and that life, once altered, was never the same again. As she read the words, a smile silently spread across her face, and she paused for a moment to try to absorb what this was going to mean. She was being assigned to a post in Boston. She had worked in an optical shop in Provo when she was married to Ed, and the army recognized that this was a useful skill that could be put to use in serving in the war efforts. She was to pack up and be prepared to leave in forty-eight hours. She was shipping out.

The months in Boston were busy and stimulating. Boston was a completely different culture from the small town in Utah, where she had grown up. There were so many historical things to see on her days of R and R, and she had found good friends during her time on the east coast. There were a lot of widows in the army in those days. She didn't feel so alone. There was a group of women that liked to stop in at the local ice cream parlor once a week, and Blanche was beginning to gain a little weight on what had been an emaciated body, when she had first decided to join the army. Good health was beginning to return.

The weekend was coming, and Blanche and several of her friends were getting a weekend pass to leave the post. They brainstormed together, and decided to take the train to New York City to see the sights. She realized that never before in her life had there been so much culture to absorb. The train was filled with men and women in uniform. Many were traveling alone, some were finding comfort in the companionship of another soldier, and some gathered together with a group of friends, forming a sort of protective barrier from all the tragedy that raged amidst the war.

The first stop was a show in the city. They were going to see the world-famous Rockettes at Radio City Music Hall. The costuming, dancing, staging and showmanship were beyond anything she had ever seen. How could they all kick their legs so high in perfect unison? She was mesmerized.

The next morning, the girls all had breakfast together at a restaurant that overlooked Rockefeller Plaza. They watched the skaters glide across the ice with grace and beauty. Blanche paused for a moment as she soaked in her setting, and she realized she was feeling something she had not recognized in her heart for a long time. She was feeling an acceptance and peace about the hand that life had dealt her. It was a peace which had come at a great expense. She knew there would never be another Edward in her life again, but she felt blessed and grateful that she had known a love such as theirs had been. It was something that could not be measured in the amount of time that they had spent together. Their love would change the rest of her life, and she knew it. Why he had been taken, and she had been left behind, she would never know. Blanche had many dreams about Ed in the months and years that followed his death. She always felt him telling her that, ultimately, things were going to be alright. Her eyes floated back to the skaters, and she quietly tucked her thoughts of Ed into a silent and holy corner of her heart. It was time to head back to the train station. Their weekend in New York City was over.

Thirteen months passed, while Blanche was stationed in Boston. She wrote to Violet often, and was always filled with excitement when she received a small, sweet letter from Melba. Violet's first son had been born, and they had named him Edwin. Her brother, J.T., was stationed in France, and she treasured the correspondence between them. Letters meant a lot during wartime. It was the lifeline to births and deaths, tragedy and peace. She knew that a change was coming, and her friends were beginning to receive new orders. Slowly, her friends were being sent to different destinations around the world.

She was called to a military meeting with several other WACS. "You're being issued cold-weather uniforms this afternoon," their Commanding Officer told them. "Report back to this same building tomorrow morning. You will receive your final orders after that. You have the rest of the afternoon off." When the women returned to their barracks, there was much speculation among them about where they were being sent. Many felt that they would be going to England. Everyone said it was a cold that sank deep into your bones when you were in London. London was the place where the blitz from Hitler's air force had decimated a once beautiful city. They had been issued wool skirts and jackets, military overcoats and boots. Anticipation surrounded the women that night, and there was little sleep, as they prepared for the enormous change that was coming. The sun came up, and a new day began. Blanche walked the short distance to the hall they had been assigned to meet in. Their Commanding Officer stood up and went to the front of the room and faced them. "You are to turn in the uniforms that you were issued yesterday, and go to the clothing hall to receive hot climate clothing. You are going to the South Pacific. You are being stationed in New Guinea."

The women never knew why they had initially been given cold weather uniforms, and the seriousness of the situation was very clear. The Philippine Islands had been filled with violence, occupation by the Japanese, and horrific stories of capture and torture had been in all the newspapers.

The next day, the women began to receive shots to try to protect them from the vile disease that was prevalent in that part of the world. Blanche returned to her bunk after receiving four shots in a single day, and fought nausea and fever the rest of the afternoon. They were boarding a ship to the South Pacific in a week. She slept restlessly throughout the night. She was sick from the shots, and her dreams were fevered and extreme. Fear and anticipation tugged at her level-headed, common sense, and she wondered what danger she was walking into. Many women were being held in P.O.W. camps in the South Pacific. Women who had been with their military husbands overseas before the invasions began, and couldn't get out in time. Women who had their ships sunk, while trying to get back to the United States, and had been picked up by the Japanese and thrown in camps to rot. Courage was not a new mentality for Blanche, and she reached deep in her soul and pulled out the fortitude that had become a part of her character.

Hundreds of women boarded the ship and found their way to their bunks. They would be on the water twenty one days without seeing land. Many of the women were desperately ill with sea sickness, and, blessedly, Blanche was not. She often went on deck, and the years of her life went through her mind like a movie. She prepared herself to land and to cope with whatever circumstances she would find herself in. The days passed.

Finally, the women stepped off the ship and onto land. It was hot. There were tropical trees and natives. There was an abundance of fresh fruit. Bananas and pineapples grew like weeds. The natives scaled the trees and cut fresh fruit for the women daily. All of the women had mosquito nets around their sleeping cots, and the environment was nothing Blanche could have ever imagined. They knew that danger was not far away, and that the Japanese were determined to control the Pacific. The months passed, and when the letters came from home it was a good day.

Blanche had finished her work for the day, and had washed out her mess kit after dinner and wandered back to the barracks. She had received a letter from Violet, and she treasured the quiet hours she had to herself to read her mail and rest. Blanche lay back on her bunk and began to read Violet's letter. She had only read a few sentences when her heart sank, and darkness seemed to close down her mind. J.T. had been shot in the arm, and it was very serious. They had shipped him back to the United States and, after several attempts to save his arm, it had been amputated. He had been in the hospital for weeks, and he continued to fight infection and complications. Blanche put her head in her hands, and a jagged sob escaped her. She thought back to the day she had sat with her brother on the porch of their farmhouse. The day that Mama had died, and Melba had been born. Blanche and J.T. had always been extremely close. She had no idea when she would ever see him again, or any of her family, for that matter. Her heart was heavy.

The sun rose on the next day, and she was required to do her duty and get through the work of the day. Days passed and, finally, she received another letter. It was a

handwriting that she had never seen before, and she quickly
opened it and began to read.

Dear Pal,

*You must be wondering how I am. Sometimes I
wonder too.*

It was from J.T. He was learning to write with his left
hand. He spent most of his time in the hospital, but he was
in Utah, and close enough for his wife and small son to be
able to come and visit him a couple of times a month.
Blanche was overjoyed to hear from him and to feel his
love and humor in his letter, despite his own overwhelming
loss. She read his letters over and over, and began to think
about when she would see him again. The war with
Germany had been won, but the war in the South Pacific
raged on. The beloved President Roosevelt had died
shortly after winning reelection to his fourth term, and the
fate of the rest of the war now lay upon President Truman.
People talked of bombs beyond comprehension finishing
the war, but no one knew if it was fact or fiction. The truth
about the holocaust had finally been exposed, after the
troops had liberated the death camps. No one had really
believed the stories could be true, until after the war, when
the extent of the atrocities had been exposed. Blanche
longed to be near her family again, and began to dream of
the day when she would see Violet, Melba, June and J.T.
Her sister June had been sick most of her life, with a type
of bronchitis that she could never get rid of. The doctors

didn't understand it very well, and medical options in the country in Utah were limited.

Blanche knew that her years in the army had given her perspective and strength, that she would draw upon throughout the rest of her life. She often sat on the beach at sunset, and watched the red sun slowly sink into the massive expanse of the ocean. She wondered what the rest of her life would be like, and longed to have a home and a place where she could bring a now teenaged Melba to live with her.

She looked down the beach and saw another female soldier running towards her. "Blanche, there is news," she cried out. "The United States just dropped an atomic bomb on Hiroshima," she said. "More than fifty thousand people were killed immediately, and thousands of others were injured. I don't know what this means," she said.

No one really knew what it meant. The world was stunned and, yet, the war continued. Days passed, and life on the island of New Guinea continued for Blanche as it had been. It was Aug 9, 1945, and the news that changed the world came. A second atomic bomb had been dropped on Nagasaki. It had flattened a square mile on impact, and again, tens of thousands of people had been killed. It was the military move that ended the war, although many throughout history would never forgive the United States for doing it. It was over. Blanche was going home.

CHAPTER FIVE: CIVILIAN LIFE

The train whistle blew as the wheels slowed to a stop in the Salt Lake City train depot. Blanche stepped from the train, impeccably dressed in a tailored navy blue suit, with matching pumps and a patent leather handbag. She carried a small suitcase in her right hand, and took a deep breath as she surveyed the dozens of people filling the train station. Some were still in uniform. Many were not and, amidst the returning soldiers, she observed scenes of loved ones reuniting, as well as the numberless soldiers struggling to find balance and dignity despite a missing arm or leg. She headed towards the information booth, to try to determine how long she would need to wait to catch a bus that would take her far from the city and back to the Uintah Valley, where she had grown up. Her thoughts wandered to the world she would find when she finally arrived home again. Dad had died in a work-related accident in 1941. Violet had two children now, and her youngest daughter, Betty, had been born during the war when Blanche was overseas. Melba was living with her stepmother, and life had been turbulent. Her brother, James Truman, was still in the hospital, where he had been for months now. His recovery from his arm amputation was still plagued with complications and setbacks. June was living with Violet for the time being, and her health had been very bad.

Her mind snapped back to the present, as she pressed forward to inquire about the bus schedule, and after determining it would be a few hours before the bus would leave, she set off to find a sandwich and a cup of tea. She sat alone amidst her thoughts and savored the sweet spice of her warm peach tea, and tried to put the events of the last three years into perspective. In a very short amount of time, she had gone from being a bride to a widow, to a soldier to a civilian. She knew she was returning to the small farming community of Hanna a much different person than when she had left for Provo to attend high school. She longed to see her sisters and her brother. She wished she could spend time with her Dad, and try to understand why he had married this woman so very different from her mother. But that was impossible; he had passed away many years ago. Loneliness, she thought, can make you do strange things.

Blanche had grown good at being alone. Of course, in the army you were never physically alone, but in many ways, the regiment and order of the army had served as a shield against the harsh realities that she had known in the twenty-four years of her life. Blanche was a beautiful and well-traveled woman now. She wasn't sure yet what she wanted to do with the rest of her life. For now, her only thoughts were of getting back to the farm, to Melba, and of creating a life, where there was more stability than the inhumane chaos that had reigned through the world during the last four years of World War II.

A soft voice broke through the stillness of her thoughts, and she turned when she heard a voice from the past say, "Blanche, is that you?" She looked up to see a uniformed Billy Turnbow, who had been a part of the three-student first grade class when she had attended school in Hanna.

"Bill," she said brightly, "When did you get in?" "I got here about an hour ago," he said. "I'm waiting for my brother Lloyd to pick me up and give me a ride back to the ranch." Blanche had heard that Bill had been serving in England. He looked quite handsome, and like he had seen a part of life that had aged him far beyond the years of the war. "How are you getting home?" he asked her. "There's a bus leaving in a couple of hours," she said. "Oh, come along with us," he replied. "We're headed to the same place, and we can catch up on old times." "Very well then," she said as she carefully placed her hankie in her handbag and snapped the gold clasp shut. "I appreciate it, and I'd love to hear what you have been doing the last few years."

Bill graciously reached down and picked up her small suitcase. "We're out this way," he said. Together they slowly made their way through the crowd and out to the loading area of the parking lot. "It's good to see you, Blanche. I'm so sorry about the loss of your husband." "Thank you," she said quietly. "Tell me how your family is doing," Bill said. The two-hour drive out of the city and through the country went by quickly, as they told each other stories of their time spent in the army. Bill had worked as a medic for much of his time in England. He listened with interest as she described her months spent in Boston, and of life in the jungles of New Guinea. Bill had always been fond of Blanche, and he never really thought he would see her again after she had moved to Provo in her teens. Blanche had once been teased by her older sister, Violet, when Billy sent her a valentine, which she was too young to read at the time, asking her to marry him. They were in first grade.

The car pulled up in front of the old farm house, and an overjoyed Melba ran down the porch stairs to embrace her sister. She was home.

CHAPTER SIX: SECOND CHANCES

Bill was a frequent visitor to the sheep farm, where Melba was living with her stepmother. Blanche loved Melba fiercely, and was glad to be home and near her once again. The handsome army vet was kind and thoughtful, and couldn't believe his good fortune to have Blanche back in the small community again, after so many years. Blanche began to think about moving forward in her life, and of having a family and a home. Bill's mother was one hundred percent Scandinavian, and Bill's fair skin and hair, combined with his attention, began to make Blanche ponder the possibility of a future with him. He certainly seemed to desire her company in his life, and the harsh realities of the years that had passed, had made Blanche become much more of a realist than she once was so many years ago.

One thing that she knew for sure, was that she was taking Melba to live with her. She had never been close to her stepmother. Her stern approach to life and parenting only reminded Blanche of all of the love that had been lost over the years. Melba was a young teenager and adored her older sisters. She had spent much of the time that Blanche had been in the army living with Violet. The loving influence of her sisters had given Melba a sweet and positive disposition, that would stay with her the rest of her life.

Blanche had learned that sometimes in life love grows quietly. While her marriage to Ed had been an intensely loving relationship, she knew that no two men or relationships were ever the same. Bill was a good and strong man, and he loved her. He understood what Blanche and her sisters had been through since the death of their mother, and he understood the world that she came from. After all, they had been two of the three students in the first grade class in Hanna. They had spent years together, as they went through their early education in the small one-room schoolhouse. Blanche felt that he could offer her a good life, and she highly respected his family. His mother was a kind and loving woman, and Blanche thought about this sweet woman becoming the grandmother of the children she might have one day. It just all made sense and seemed to naturally fall into place.   It was Saturday evening, and Blanche packed a small suitcase with enough clothes for a couple of days. She gathered Melba into her arms and told her she was going to be gone for a few days, but she would be back soon.

That evening, Bill pulled up in front of the farmhouse, and Blanche quietly walked out into the spring evening and climbed into the car. They were headed to Reno. They were eloping.

Chapter Seven: David

Blanche and Bill settled into their first home in Provo. Bill was attending college there, and it was a kind of charmed community. Melba lived with them, and they were a contented little family. Soon, the miracle of a new life would be joining them, and Blanche began to believe that life was going to have order and love, and she cherished that.

David William Turnbow was born June 8, 1947. He was fair and Nordic like his Father, and was the joy of their lives. Melba adored David, and would rock him for hours as she told him stories and sang to him. Life had meaning and goodness and love for all of them. David grew, and the months passed quickly as he learned to crawl and take his first steps.

He was a year old, and Bill and Blanche were going back to Hanna to celebrate the Fourth of July with his family. It was a fun day spending time with Bill's brothers and his sister and their families. All of Bill's brothers had married WWII widows. It was a strange twist of fate. The war had caused so much injury and loss, and people were ready to live again. As children began to be born, the sting of death was not as acute.

After several hours of visiting and enjoying a meal together, Bill and Blanche began to load up the car and prepare for the drive home. David had fallen asleep in the late afternoon, and Blanche gently climbed into the back seat with him, where there would be more room for him to stretch out and sleep comfortably. They said good-bye and headed back to Provo to spend the evening with Melba.

It was a dusty country road, and the sun was shining softly through the window at the end of a pleasant afternoon. Blanche never saw the truck coming. She was lost in her sweet thoughts about her sleeping baby, and also filled with joy to have found out that she was expecting another child.

They went around the point of the mountain, and Bill suddenly yelled a fierce primal sort of scream, that was strangled and lost in the sound of breaking glass and twisted metal. They had been hit head-on by a drunk driver. The last thing Blanche saw, before she was swallowed by the blanket of darkness, was the face of her precious child.

CHAPTER EIGHT: THE ACCIDENT

Amazingly, Bill, who had been driving, was the least injured. In fact, he did not even realize that his finger had been cut off, until he went to get a drink of water at the hospital and saw the end of his finger barely attached. Blanche was in critical condition. The front seat had completely detached and landed on the back seat. David was taken immediately to Primary Children's Hospital in Salt Lake City, where they performed brain surgery that night. When he came out of surgery, Bill's mother Louise was in the recovery room waiting for him. It was extremely serious, and the doctors gave little hope that he would live. Louise softly walked over to the crib that held the bandaged and bruised baby boy that was her grandson. She put her finger in the palm of his hand and, despite the trauma he had just been through, he grabbed a hold of it, even as he lay unconscious. She was a woman of deep faith, and the storms of life were blowing. She prayed mightily for the life of this child to be spared, and she waited. Hours passed, but she never left his side. The dark night sky was beginning to lighten with the break of day, and the sun was starting to rise as if it had no idea what had just happened to this family. She watched his little chest fighting to breathe, but David never opened his eyes again.

His little hand wrapped around the finger of his loving Norwegian Grandmother slowly began to lose its grip and, as a new day began, David slipped away to a Heavenly realm. He had just turned one, and he was gone. How would they ever carry the grief?

Bill's brother Lloyd solemnly walked down the hallway of the Provo hospital to find his brother. It was very early in the morning, and the decision had been made for him to be the one to tell Bill that his first born child was dead. Bill was sitting in the waiting room with his head in his hands, sick with worry over his wife and son. Blanche had received severe head injuries and the doctors did not know if she was going to survive.

Bill jumped to his feet as he saw Lloyd approaching. He desperately tried to read his brothers eyes for a hint of his son's condition. Lloyd somehow choked out the inconceivable words and Bill collapsed. A nurse was at his side immediately, and the doctor gently tried to revive him. Bill opened his eyes, but he could see nothing but darkness. The words that were being spoken seemed to come from far away, and he could not comprehend what he was being told. His world was shattered. His son was dead and his wife was in critical condition.

Melba arrived at the hospital and embraced her brother-in-law. "We will find a way to survive this, Bill," she said gently, as they sat and listened to the doctor speak. He told them that under no condition could they tell Blanche that her son had passed away, or the shock of it would kill her too. How could they ever look at her and tell her this lie. They would do it to try to keep her alive. Right now, that was the only thing there was left to fight for.

Violet arrived at the hospital some hours later, as soon as she could make arrangements to get transportation from the valley into the city. Melba ran to her and burst into tears. "I had to go in to Blanche and tell her that David was going to be okay. It was the first thing she asked about after regaining consciousness. It was the hardest thing I have ever done in my whole life, but I did it to try to keep her alive." Violet, who was no stranger to life's violent and staggering losses, held her sister in her arms as she wept inconsolably. There was something else. The baby that Blanche was carrying had died in the crash too. There was no fetal heartbeat.

Three days passed, and the decision to wait on holding David's funeral had been made due to the gravity of his mother's condition. The doctors finally told Bill that it was time to tell her. A nurse entered the room first and gave Blanche an injection for pain, and to alter her awareness, as if a blanket had been thrown over her sense of reality and her emotions. She heard the words, and she heard the scream that she knew came from deep within her. Within a few minutes, everything closed in around her, and she passed out. She lived a state of altered delirium, knowing that she had been told her son was dead, and fighting the pain of having her scalp completely torn off her head and sewn back on again.

Slowly, Blanche began to wake up and understand the impact of what had happened. She was ill. She was so very, very ill. Violet held her hand and told her she would live through this, and she would go on with her life. Gradually, they began to try to get her up, because they knew the fetus was going to pass from her, and the miscarriage was yet another thing that she must bear. Life was dark for a long, long time.

Chapter Nine: Aftermath

Blanche weighed under a hundred pounds when, weeks later, she was wheeled out of the hospital to be released to go home. She was a broken woman, and deeply depressed. As Bill helped her into the car, she saw the small bouquet of flowers in the back seat. She had missed her son's funeral, but she would not go home until she had seen his grave and said goodbye to her only child. It was a desolate time for Bill and Blanche. The weeks passed, and Blanche was still gravely ill. She had been diagnosed with a type of blood poisoning, and the doctors needed to reopen the wound on her head to try to clear out infection. She was going back into the hospital.

It was discovered during the surgery, that the emergency room doctor working the night of the accident was so sure that she would not survive, that he had sewn her head back together without ever cleaning out the wound. They found not only gravel, but a bobby pin that had been sewn back into her head. The doctor who had committed this atrocity lost his license to ever practice medicine again. That did little to help Blanche to heal and to fight for her life.

Months passed, and Blanche began to regain her strength. Bill and Blanche were overwhelmed with medical bills from the car accident. Insurance was not the same in those days, and they would be receiving no financial compensation from the other party. The cost of David's brain surgery and Blanche's extended stay in the hospital were staggering. They were left with few options. They would have to sell their house to pay the hospital bills. Months later, when the house had sold and the hospital bills had been paid, they were left with just enough money to buy a small trailer house. Life was torture right then for the young couple. Every time Blanche left the house to buy groceries or do an errand, she ran into well-meaning friends who tried to comfort her, but it was like constantly having the scab ripped off a deep sore. Finally, Bill came home one afternoon to find Blanche holding a soft blue sweater that had been David's. She was lost in a sorrow too deep to bear. She sobbed in her husband's arms, with an anguish she had never known.

Bill gently pulled an afghan over his wife when, eventually, she fell into a troubled sleep. He walked outside and looked at the night sky, and tried to sort out in his mind how they were ever going to get beyond this. Men in those days didn't talk about their feelings, and Bill repressed a sorrow and rage that would plague him for the rest of his life. He knew they had to leave. He had to get his wife away from this familiar place, where they were so well-known, and the tragedy that they had just been through was constantly fresh. They would take the trailer, and they would travel for a while. He would find small jobs to sustain them along the way, and, hopefully, one day they would believe that a decent future might lie ahead for them. He was far from convinced himself, but he felt this was the right thing to do for himself and his wife.

Two weeks later, Bill and Blanche pulled out of town and began to distance themselves from the place where their son was buried. They would stop for a few weeks or a month in California, Oregon and Washington, and during that time, Blanche would call Violet to try to stay in touch with her sisters and her brother.

They had been on the road for six months, and it was the beginning of 1948. Blanche walked to the pay phone down the street from the small trailer park that they were stopped in. She dropped the coins in the phone and waited to hear Violet answer with her sweet familiar voice. Violet's voice was different today when she said hello. Blanche knew immediately that something was wrong. "It's June," Violet said. "She is going in to have surgery on her lung, and her condition is serious." J.T. was also not showing the signs of improvement that the doctors were hoping for, and Blanche knew that Violet was worried.

That evening, Bill and Blanche shared a simple meal of steak, potatoes and salad and quietly discussed the situation. Perhaps it was time to go back to Provo, so that Blanche could see her brother again, and be there when her sister came out of surgery. The decision to travel for a while had been a good one. They had seen a part of the United States that neither of them had been familiar with, and Bill was very impressed with the golden State of California, and the booming employment opportunities there seemed to be in the state that overlooked the Pacific Ocean. He tucked these thoughts away in a quiet corner of his mind, as he and his wife made the decision to begin the trip back to Utah. Blanche's health had grown stronger during the last six months, and he knew that she missed her brother and her sisters.

They arrived in Salt Lake City the day before June's surgery. Blanche gently knocked on the hospital door, as she quietly walked into her sister's room. June looked gray, and Blanche was deeply concerned. In the hour that passed as they talked, June told Blanche that she didn't believe that she would be coming out of the surgery alive. Blanche reassured her that things were going to be alright, and that she and Violet would be waiting for her when she woke up. Blanche gently squeezed her hand just before the nurses came to wheel her into the operating room. Together Bill, Blanche and Violet waited for the doctor to emerge from surgery. Three hours later, a doctor approached them, and they knew before he opened his mouth to speak. June had been right. They had lost their sister, and they had to go from Salt Lake City to Provo to tell J.T.

They walked down the hospital corridor together and entered their brother's room. J.T. was still so handsome in spite of his missing arm, and his humor had never diminished, despite what he had endured. Softly, Violet broke the news to him, and James Truman fell into a deep state of sorrow. They sat with him for an hour, and he began to look very tired, so they stood up to leave for a while to let him rest. Violet and Blanche were at his hospital door, just as they turned and saw him clutch his chest. He had suffered a severe heart attack. James lived for five more days, and in a week's time, Blanche and Violet buried both J.T. and June.

CHAPTER TEN: SUNRISE

It was the summer of 1949. Blanche slowly emerged from their small trailer, and sat down in a lawn chair to enjoy the peacefulness of the summer morning. Her hand instinctively moved to her swollen belly, as she felt the warm sunlight on her face. She and Bill were expecting a baby in November. She loved this time of the morning by herself, when she softly spoke to her unborn child, and wondered at the miracle of life perpetuating itself, despite all of the efforts of adversity to stain optimism. Blanche had been in good health throughout her pregnancy, and she and Bill were settled in Provo. Bill had begun working with a construction company that paid well, and always had work. They had many job sites throughout the United States, and even into Canada. The economy in the United States was booming.

Blanche began to buy things for the new baby, who she would be holding in her arms in just a few months. Tiny yellow nightgowns and undershirts were tucked into a dresser drawer, and the movement of new life within her brought joy into a corner of her heart that had shut down when David died. She passed the hours that Bill was at work knitting and sewing and preparing for the new baby. Blanche had tiny little hands, and had always been

extremely talented when it came to intricate stitchery, and
was a self-taught tailor. Many friends and neighbors would
come by if they had any questions about a sewing project,
and Blanche always instinctively knew how to solve the
problem, and she enjoyed the creative fulfillment.

Summer slowly faded into the rich colors of fall, and
Provo was beautiful, with the trees drenched in golden
crimson autumn colors. It was a chilly November morning,
and Blanche moved slowly in her ninth month of
pregnancy. She noticed a slight cramping that morning, but
having given birth once before she knew that her body was
probably just preparing for the great act of childbirth. A
couple of hours later, she realized the cramping was
increasing and starting to come at regular intervals. She
glanced at herself in the mirror and spoke to the strong
woman, who had endured much and still managed to keep
her heart open to love. "Well, here we go," she said to
herself. She gently woke Bill and told him it was time to
go to the hospital.

Donna Rae Turnbow was born November 22, 1949. She
was a beautiful, healthy baby girl, and Bill and Blanche
loved her deeply. She was a happy baby and, soon after her
birth and Blanche's subsequent recovery, they moved into a
house that they had been able to buy. Life was starting
over for them. A picture of David hung in their bedroom
throughout the rest of their marriage, but life had meaning
for them again now, and together with their precious baby
girl, they were once again a family embarking on a
promising future.

Donna resembled her mother with her dark hair and beautifully sculpted face. With the loss of David, Blanche had quietly hoped to give birth to a daughter during her pregnancy. She never took one second of motherhood for granted, and the days when Donna was an infant and toddler were joyful. Bill was working for a construction company doing massive cement work on dams, freeways and a variety of large projects. They were transferred several times and lived in North Dakota, British Columbia, Canada, and, eventually, back in California.

It was January of 1954, and Bill and Blanche were living in Albany, California. It was in the San Francisco Bay area that their second daughter, Lynne Louise Turnbow, was born on January 26, 1954. Blanche was overjoyed to have two daughters. Lynne was fair and Nordic, as David had been.

Bill loved his daughters and his wife. He worked hard, but he was also tortured throughout the rest of his life by the loss of his son. He began to drink, and it took a heavy toll on the lives of his family over the decades ahead.

Bill and Blanche finally settled for a long stretch of time in Pleasant Hill, California. They were about twenty miles from San Francisco, and when they had relatives who would come to visit them, Bill would often give them the "Five Dollar Tour," or the "Ten Dollar Tour," of the beautiful city that they lived in such close proximity to. Bill was meticulous in his care of the yards and property in each house that they owned.

Blanche stepped into the backyard on a warm summer afternoon and surveyed her setting. They lived on Shelly Drive, in a little neighborhood frequently referred to as "Poets Corner." All the streets were named after well-known writers. They had a large yard with several fruit trees, berry bushes and a garden, from which they would harvest delicious summer vegetables. Blanche spent hours in her kitchen in the summer canning fruit and making jam. Sometimes they would play croquet in the backyard with their daughters, and Blanche felt blessed in many ways to have a family and a home. Making that work, at whatever the, cost meant more to her than anything else.

There were good memories over the years that tempered some of the adversity in her marriage. For several years, Bill would take his family to the Rheem Valley Theatre on Sunday afternoons to watch an afternoon matinee. It was an Old-Hollywood type of theater, with murals and deep rich carpets. Ushers wearing uniforms and carrying flashlights would show you to your seat. Bill liked eating nice dinners at fancy restaurants in San Francisco, and one of his favorite spots came with a sweeping vista of the Pacific Ocean.

After several years on Shelly Drive, Bill and Blanche bought a larger home that sat on top of a hill in a beautiful neighborhood. Bill's mother, Louise, would take the Trailways bus from Salt Lake City to San Francisco, and stay with her son and his family for several weeks each year. There were many car trips to Utah, during the years their daughters were growing up. Both Bill's and

Blanche's siblings had remained, for the most part, in Utah. While Donna and Lynne lived several states away from their only Grandparent, her incredible sweet love still permeated their lives on the occasions that they had with her, and she was a wonderful and stable influence in their lives.

Blanche was involved for many years in various church activities. Each year, the ward she was in had a bazaar, where they sold handmade items to raise money. She often donated a handmade afghan, and her quilts and blankets were always detailed and meticulous. She worked with the children of the ward in Primary, and would always make cupcakes on the day of the month that they had the five-cent cupcake sale.

During their years in Pleasant Hill, The Oakland Temple was built, and they had the opportunity to tour the temple before its dedication. It was a stunning sight, and their daughters were able to participate in numerous large youth-oriented church activities during those years.

Blanche watched history unfold, as the country coped with the assassination of President John Kennedy, Martin Luther King, Jr., and Robert Kennedy. Families were divided, as the United States became more deeply entrenched in the Viet Nam War. Women began to demand equal pay for equal work performed alongside their male coworkers. People sat on their porches on warm summer evenings, as men walked on the moon for the first time.

Bill was injured in a serious work-related accident when he was in his forties. A construction worker, driving a big rig loaded with thousands of pounds of steel, had stopped to ask for directions. Somehow, as he drove away, there was a terrible mix-up, and Bill's legs became tangled in the double set of wheels. His legs were run over twice. He spent an entire summer in the hospital and, at one point, amputation was a consideration. Eventually, he was released and was able to do some construction work in the years ahead, but he was permanently affected by the damage done to his legs, and suffered a lot of pain throughout the rest of his life from his injuries.

The girls were growing up, and Blanche knew that one day they would leave and have lives of their own. She did not look forward to that time, but she began to learn the art of aging with grace, as she watched her daughters graduate from high school and begin college. A new time of life had now begun for Blanche and, bravely, she walked forward, as she had learned to do throughout her entire life.

CHAPTER ELEVEN: SUNSET

It was 1977, and Lynne would soon be giving birth to Blanche's first grandchild. Born three weeks late, Elizabeth Anne Borges came into this world as an adored, desired and loved baby. In the next five years, four more granddaughters would be born, who would know Blanche as their grandmother. Donna was the mother of three beautiful girls, and Lynne was the mother of two. Donna lived in upstate New York for ten years, and Blanche traveled to the East Coast to visit her daughter and granddaughters several times. Lynne remained in California, while raising her children on the beautiful Central Coast. Her daughters grew up building sand castles and watching majestic sunsets into the vast blue ocean.

Bill and Blanche moved from Pleasant Hill, after both of their daughters had married and moved away. They spent a couple of years living in the Sierra Nevada Foothills, ten years in Central California, two years close to her youngest daughter Lynne, and the last move of their lives was to Seattle, to be near to Donna.

Blanche shifted slightly in her hospital bed, as Donna sat nearby speaking quietly to her. She had been admitted the night before for severe back pain. She had developed osteoporosis in her sixties, and had fractured three vertebrae in her back. The morphine had not eased the pain, and the doctors were unsure why it had not. Donna was leaving for about an hour to pick up her little girls at school and feed them lunch. Blanche said that she was tired and was just going to lie back and rest for a while, but that she would see Donna again in the afternoon.

Blanche closed her eyes and a beautiful dream began to wrap its arms around her. She was a young woman again, walking with strength and purpose, just as she had learned to do in the military. She held her head high and walked forward through a tunnel towards the light that she could see ahead. She was free of pain and felt a weightless freedom and ease. As she neared the end of the tunnel, she began to see a host of people dressed in white, who all seemed to be waiting for her. She stepped forward into the light, and a peace and calm defying earthly explanation permeated her. A woman stood ahead of the rest waiting for her. Blanche took a step forward and quietly spoke one word, "Mama." She had been twelve years old when her mother died, and had lived her entire adult life without the love and presence of this adoring woman. Maude Ivie Rose was the first to greet her, and Blanche fell into her arms. To be a daughter again was an eternal comfort.

There was soon a great reunion. They were all there waiting for her. Her precious son David, J.T., June, Dad and a strikingly handsome gentleman she recognized as Edward. As she walked forward surrounded by a sea of love, she soon saw the beautiful Nordic face of Louise

Turnbow. The sweet woman who had been the only grandparent her daughters had known. How she had loved and appreciated each of these people in her lifetime.

They moved forward towards a City of Light, and Blanche realized that her earthly journey had come to an end, and that she was on the other side of The Holy Passage. Her spirit would return to Earth often over the next year, although time is measured only as an earthly concept. She lived in a world just adjacent to her loved ones still on Earth, and she surrounded them with her holy light and strength, as they continued to live their lives. She had finished her work on Earth. Now, a new journey was beginning.

CHAPTER TWELVE: POSTERITY

Lynne stepped out of the plane and made her way towards the Baggage Claim Area. Her eyes searched the crowd for her sister and, finally, their eyes connected, and they were reunited. Donna had flown in from Seattle and Lynne from her home in California, and they were meeting at the Salt Lake City Airport. Blanche had passed away over twenty years ago, and their father just a few years later.

They had made this incredible journey into Utah to see their beloved Aunt Violet, who had long since outlived all of her siblings by decades. Even Melba had passed over to the other side now after living to marry, give birth to five children and become a grandmother.

Donna herself was a grandmother now, and Lynne's two daughters were both professional women in their thirties. Aunt Violet had devoted her life not only to loving her own six children, but to staying in touch and deeply loving her siblings' children, as, one by one, all of her sisters and brother passed through the veil.

Violet had been widowed twice in her lifetime, and had lost her oldest son to cancer. When Violet was in her eighties, the home that she had lived in for over fifty years caught fire one night and burned down. Still, her work on Earth was not finished, and she lingered. She wondered many times why she had lived so much longer than her sisters and brother. She was adored by her children, grand-children, great-grandchildren, great-great-grandchildren, nieces and nephews.

Violet had been gravely ill, and her own children had gathered at her bedside and stayed with her for weeks. When beyond all medical explanation she lived through this very serious episode, her children reluctantly had to begin going home, and back to their families and jobs.

Donna and Lynne had made the decision to fly into Utah to see her, knowing that it would probably be the last time they would have to be with her. They quickly got into a taxi and headed towards the hotel near Temple Square. It was almost midnight by the time they both got to Utah after unexpected flight delays. The next day, they would rent a car and travel to Salem, Utah, where Aunt Violet was now living.

It was late May, and the weather was still rainy and chilly. The snow line on the mountains was low, and spring had come late this year to Utah. They would have two precious days with their Aunt before they had to go home, and they were grateful for any time with her, considering how sick she had been and how precarious her health continued to be.

Lynne gently pushed the door open and wrapped her Aunt into her arms. It had been nineteen years since they had seen each other. It was a long afternoon filled with family stories and memories. Holding Aunt Violet's hand was like holding their mother's hand. Blanche and Violet had endured and thrived through so much in their lives. They had lived through history that changed the world. Aunt Violet had been the last surviving Rose sister for almost twenty years, and she was cherished. As the evening drew to a close, Donna and Lynne left to return to their hotel. They would have one more day with her.

The next day they were joined by daughters of both Violet and Melba. The light broke through the cloudy sky and danced off the intense white snow on the mountains. Though the four women representing the next generation of Rose women lived very divergent lives, they were united in that moment by their shared history and their love for Aunt Violet. The hours passed, and Violet rested. Donna, Lynne and their cousins spoke of all who had come and gone in their family line, and of the profound effect of these three sisters on all the children, grandchildren and great-grandchildren who were their descendants. It was a day written on the pages of eternity, and it was coming to an end. With great anguish, Donna and Lynne held their Aunt one final time and said good-bye. It was a quiet ride returning to Salt Lake City. They would have a few hours in the morning before catching their flights home, and they had decided to walk around the Temple Grounds before taking a taxi to the airport.

Saturday morning was warm and lovely, and there was great comfort in their final hours together. They sat in the shadow of the beautiful Salt Lake City Temple with full hearts. It was a place of great peace and beauty, with the pristine flowers and the beautiful brides who kept emerging from the temple. The story of the pioneers, who had weathered incredible hardship to come to this land and build this city, was inspiring. It was a time of looking both forward and back. They had been profoundly affected by this opportunity to reach back into their own family history, and their mother's light and influence felt close by.

The weather was a perfect seventy degrees, with a gentle warm breeze. Lynne felt the whisper of angels, as her hair gently caught the breeze. How can the importance and value of one life be measured? The story of her mother's life danced through her mind. Lynne thought of the family history that she had shared with her own daughters, and of the importance of the story continuing to be told. We are all given time at birth. How much time we will have, none of us know. For David, it was short. For Violet, the years had stretched nearly to a century. The hardships we will be asked to bear, and the unexpected mercies we are shown during times of distress, these things rest in God's hands.

What are we to learn from the great women who have lived and loved before us, who are our ancestors? That the power of one is great, and that the power of love is immeasurable. That one Aunt Liddy, holding a two-month premature infant in her arms, blessed countless lives who would come from this tiny baby. That the will to persevere, when one has lost a husband and an infant son, will be remembered for generations, and strengthen others when their own will to live is weak. That we are all given a gift, and perhaps our quest in life is to share it, in a way that reflects the Creator from which it came. It is important to know the women who have lived before us. It helps us know who we are, because they are a part of us in more ways than we can understand. So, this is the story of one Little Rose Girl, and of those that she loved, and those who live now because of her. We thank you for your story, your life and your love, which is the greatest gift of your legacy. We will tell your story. It will not be forgotten.... and we will meet you on the other side.... at Heaven's Gate.

EPILOGUE

It was less than two weeks after completing this manuscript that Violet Emiline Rose Lazenby Middleton made her final journey home. She died peacefully in her daughters' arms. And so, the story of one family has come full circle. Dana Rose and Maude Ivie married and grew a family, and all of those people have lived their lives and passed on to the next realm of our eternal progression.

When speaking with her daughter Joy, following her mother's death, she told me that her mother had made reference to wanting to see Blanche three times in the week before she died. I am sure, beyond a doubt, that wish has now come true.